CA… DERS

I-Spy Books
12 Star Road, Partridge Green
Horsham, Sussex RH13 8RA

CAR NUMBERS

If you want to make a car or bus journey fly by, then how about playing the numbers game. One player starts at A and the other at X, and both try to get to the other end of the alphabet in order, using the letter at the end of the number. It can be very exciting because one starts off very quickly and slows down, while the other starts very slowly and speeds up.

I have always hoped that I would see DAV 1D.
The registration number tells you a lot about the car, how old it is and in which area of the country it was registered. And it's all here in I-SPY Car Numbers.

SCORING

Scoring in I-SPY Car Numbers is by noting down letter combinations, as explained on the opposite page. Each different one you see is worth 10 points, so when you have seen 125 you will have scored 1,250 points and may award yourself the rank of CAR NUMBER SPY with Silver Honours. When you have seen 150 marks and scored 1,500 points you will be entitled to the rank of CAR NUMBER SPY with Gold Honours; you may then send your book to me, and I shall return it to you stamped with my personal seal. Your certificate of rank is on the inside-back-cover of this book.
Good hunting!

THE PRESENT SYSTEM

We can't quite match the 160 million vehicles on the roads of the USA, but when you're stuck in a traffic jam it may well feel as though all Britain's 18 million are in there with you too! And what better time than when you're in a jam, to start Spying *registration marks*, as they are properly called.

All powered vehicles that go on the road must by law have a mark, made up of letters and numbers. This book can tell you where any British-registered vehicle comes from, and probably how old it is.

If you see A1 (on the front cover) look up A in the alphabetical list and write A1 beside it. Similarly, AA1 on the back cover goes in against AA in the list. But most registrations you see will have a set of three letters. Here you omit the *first* letter, and look up the *other two* in the list, and then write down the full registration mark, both letters and numbers, against the appropriate two-letter code in the alphabetical list.

For an example take my number on the inside front cover . . . Knock off the 'C' (first letter), look up 'BR' (second two letters) in the alphabetical list, and what do you find?

—That a car dating from after 1974 (which mine is) was registered in Durham. Phew! That's a relief, because that's where I thought I did it!

But what about the suffix, the 'S' in my case, that's tacked on after the three figures? ....

Well, by 1963 we were running out of straight 3-figure numbers for vehicles, so the present system was introduced: Seven symbols made up of 3 letters, followed by up to 3 numbers, followed by a suffix letter that changed each year.

"A"	indicates	registration	in 1963
"B"	"	"	" 1964
"C"	"	"	" 1965
"D"	"	"	" 1966
"E"	"	"	" January to July 1967
"F"	"	"	" after 1st August 1967
"G"	"	"	" after 1st August 1968
"H"	"	"	" after 1st August 1969
"J"	"	"	" after 1st August 1970
"K"	"	"	" after 1st August 1971
"L"	"	"	" after 1st August 1972
"M"	"	"	" after 1st August 1973
"N"	"	"	" after 1st August 1974
"P"	"	"	" after 1st August 1975
"R"	"	"	" after 1st August 1976
"S"	"	"	" after 1st August 1977
"T"	"	"	" after 1st August 1978
"V"	"	"	" after 1st August 1979
"W"	"	"	" after 1st August 1980
"X"	"	"	" after 1st August 1981
"Y"	"	"	" after 1st August 1982

Y indicates registration up to 31st July, 1983.

And after that? A complete reversal. From the 1st of August 1983 the suffix became a prefix, tacked on the front, and new plates now have this layout:

A123 BCD

When the 4-figure system was all used up, the County and County Borough Councils who issued registrations had to change the system. A prefix letter was put in front of the existing two letters (which is why you ignore the first letter when tracing registrations for your alphabetical list) and the figures went only from 1 to 999. After that, the whole lot were reversed, with the numbers preceding the letters.

Then came the present suffixes, issued since 1974 by Local Vehicle Licensing Offices.

So there we are. Here now is the full British list with old and new registration places.

Here's one car that won't help your score, because it *never* carries a number. A car used officially by Her Majesty the Queen carries her Standard but no registration plate.

REGISTRATION AUTHORITIES AND OFFICES

	Up to Sept. 1974	Write the registration you saw in full in this column	After Oct. 1974
A	London	....	—
AA	Hampshire	....	Salisbury
AB	Worcestershire	....	Worcester
AC	Warwickshire	....	Coventry
AD	Gloucestershire	....	Gloucester
AE	Bristol	....	Bristol
AF	Cornwall	....	Truro
AG	Ayrshire	....	Kingston-upon-Hull
AH	Norfolk	....	Norwich
AI	Meath	....	Meath
AJ	Yorkshire N.R.	....	Middlesbrough
AK	Bradford	....	Sheffield
AL	Nottinghamshire	....	Nottingham
AM	Wiltshire	....	Swindon
AN	London 65—	....	Reading
	West Ham —65	....	
AO	Cumberland	....	Carlisle
AP	East Sussex	....	Brighton
AR	Hertfordshire	....	Chelmsford
AS	Nairnshire	....	Inverness
AT	Kingston-upon-Hull	....	Kingston-upon-Hull
AU	Nottingham	....	Nottingham
AV	Aberdeenshire	....	Peterborough
AW	Shropshire	....	Shrewsbury
AX	Monmouthshire	....	Cardiff
AY	Leicestershire	....	Leicester
AZ	Central Office Coleraine	....	Belfast

Here's the car with that marvellous number on the front cover, now owned by Dunlop.

Registrations were first given to vehicles on 1st November 1903, after the 1903 Road Traffic Act had received the Royal Assent. In those days they were of one or two letters followed by numbers from 1 to 9999, and Earl Russell, the first owner of A1, is said to have queued all night to be sure of getting it!

The rear cover's AA1 used to be on an old Chater Lea motorcycle but is now on this 1904 RENAULT owned by the AUTOMOBILE ASSOCIATION (of course!). Look out for it at old car rallies.

Up to Sept. 1974		Write the registration you saw in full in this column	After Oct. 1974
B	Lancashire	....	—
BA	Salford	....	Manchester
BB	Newcastle upon Tyne	....	Newcastle upon Tyne
BC	Leicester	....	Leicester
BD	Northamptonshire	....	Northampton
BE	Lindsey (Lincs.)	....	Grimsby
BF	Staffordshire	....	Stoke-on-Trent
BG	Birkenhead	....	Liverpool
BH	Buckinghamshire	....	Luton
BI	Monaghan	....	Monaghan
BJ	East Suffolk	....	Ipswich
BK	Portsmouth	....	Portsmouth
BL	Berkshire	....	Reading
BM	Bedfordshire	....	Luton
BN	Bolton	....	Bolton
BO	Cardiff	....	Cardiff
BP	West Sussex	....	Portsmouth
BR	Sunderland	....	Durham
BS	Orkney	....	Kirkwall
BT	Yorkshire E.R.	....	York
BU	Oldham	....	Manchester
BV	Blackburn	....	Preston
BW	Oxfordshire	....	Oxford
BX	Carmarthenshire	....	Haverfordwest
BY	London 65—	....	London N.W.
	Croydon —65	....	
BZ	Central Office Coleraine	....	Down

Is there an AAA1? Yes, very appropriately it went to the Marquess of Exeter, an Olympic Gold medal-winning hurdler in 1928 who later became President of the Amateur Athletic Association.

	Up to Sept. 1974	Write the registration you saw in full in this column	After Oct. 1974
C	Yorkshire W.R.	....	—
CA	Denbighshire	....	Chester
CB	Blackburn	....	Bolton
CC	Caernarvonshire	....	Bangor
CD	Brighton	....	Brighton
CE	Cambridgeshire & Isle of Ely 65—	....	Cambridge
	Cambridgeshire —65		
CF	West Suffolk	....	Reading
CG	Hampshire	....	Salisbury
CH	Derby	....	Nottingham
CI	Laoighis	....	Laois
CJ	Herefordshire	....	Hereford
CK	Preston	....	Preston
CL	Norwich	....	Norwich
CM	Birkenhead	....	Liverpool
CN	Gateshead	....	Newcastle upon Tyne
CO	Plymouth	....	Plymouth
CP	Halifax	....	Huddersfield
CR	Southampton	....	Portsmouth
CS	Ayrshire	....	Ayr
CT	Kesteven (Lincs.)	....	Boston
CU	South Shields	....	Newcastle upon Tyne
CV	Cornwall	....	Truro
CW	Burnley	....	Preston
CX	Huddersfield	....	Huddersfield
CY	Swansea	....	Swansea
		....	(except SCY: Truro for Scillies)
CZ	Central Office Coleraine	....	Belfast

Cherished numbers, as they are called, come in all shapes and sizes of car. In one morning I saw 1066AD—nice number! on a Rolls-Royce, and CR1 on a Fiat Panda.

If your Dad's car is a Triumph TR4, what better registration mark than this?

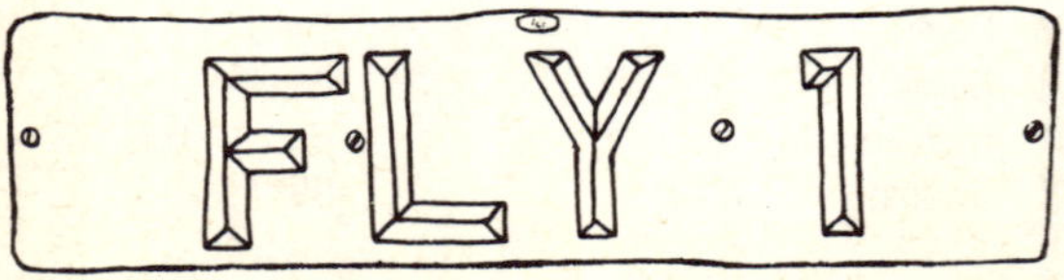

Another appropriate registration owned by the late Lord Brabazon, the first man, in 1910, to hold a Royal Aero Club Flying Certificate. Later held by Sir Freddie Laker.

	Up to Sept. 1974	Write the registration you saw in full in this column	After Oct. 1974
D	Kent	....	—
DA	Wolverhampton	....	Birmingham
DB	Stockport	....	Manchester
DC	Teesside, 68—	....	Middlesbrough
	Middlesbrough —68	....	
DD	Gloucestershire	....	Gloucester
DE	Pembrokeshire	....	Haverfordwest
DF	Gloucestershire	....	Gloucester
DG	Gloucestershire	....	Gloucester
DH	Walsall	....	Dudley
DI	Roscommon	....	Roscommon
DJ	St Helens	....	Warrington
DK	Rochdale	....	Bolton
DL	Isle of Wight	....	Newport (I.o.W.)
DM	Flintshire	....	Chester
DN	York	....	York
DO	Holland (Lincs.)	....	Boston
DP	Reading	....	Reading
DR	Plymouth 15—	....	Plymouth
	Devonport —15	....	
DS	Peeblesshire	....	Glasgow
DT	Doncaster	....	Sheffield
DU	Coventry	....	Coventry
DV	Devon	....	Exeter
DW	Newport (Mon.)	....	Cardiff
DX	Ipswich	....	Ipswich
DY	Hastings	....	Hastings
DZ	Central Office Coleraine	....	Antrim

	Up to Sept. 1974	Write the registration you saw in full in this column	After Oct. 1974
E	Staffordshire	....	—
EA	West Bromwich	....	Dudley
EB	Cambridgeshire &	....	
	Isle of Ely 65—	....	Cambridge
	Isle of Ely —65	....	
EC	Westmorland	....	Kendal
ED	Warrington	....	Warrington
EE	Grimsby	....	Grimsby
EF	Hartlepool 67—	....	Middlesbrough
	West Hartlepool —67	....	
EG	Huntingdon &	....	
	Peterborough 65—	....	Peterborough
	Peterborough —65	....	
EH	Stoke-on-Trent 10—	....	Stoke-on-Trent
	Hanley —10	....	
EI	Sligo	....	Sligo
EJ	Cardiganshire	....	Aberystwyth
EK	Wigan	....	Warrington
EL	Bournemouth	....	Bournemouth
EM	Bootle	....	Liverpool
EN	Bury	....	Bolton
EO	Barrow-in-Furness	....	Barrow-in-Furness
EP	Montgomeryshire	....	Swansea
ER	Cambridgeshire &	....	
	Isle of Ely 65—	....	Cambridge
	Cambridgeshire —65	....	
ES	Perthshire	....	Dundee
ET	Rotherham	....	Sheffield
EU	Breconshire	....	Bristol
EV	Essex	....	Chelmsford
EW	Huntingdon &	....	
	Peterborough 65—	....	Peterborough
	Huntingdonshire —65	....	
EX	Great Yarmouth	....	Norwich
EY	Anglesey	....	Bangor
EZ	Central Office Coleraine	....	Belfast

Rover VAT 69 belongs to the VAT 69 whisky distillers, and is here seen with the Forth Bridge in the background.

Space below for your own cherished number Spyings

....	....
....	....
....	....
....	....
....	....
....	....
....	....
....	....
....	....
....	....

And it's not just car numbers you can score with.

Buses are built to last, and are regularly serviced, so it's no surprise to see quite old numbers on them.

Those little tractor tugs that pull luggage and mail-bag trolleys around at big railway stations have engines, and have to go on public roads, so even they have registration marks.

	Up to Sept. 1974	Write the registration you saw in full in this column	After Oct. 1974
F	Essex	....	—
FA	Burton-upon-Trent	....	Stoke-on-Trent
FB	Bath	....	Bristol
FC	Oxford	....	Oxford
FD	Dudley	....	Dudley
FE	Lincoln	....	Lincoln
FF	Merionethshire	....	Aberystwyth
FG	Fifeshire	....	Brighton
FH	Gloucester	....	Gloucester
FI	Tipperary (N. Riding)	....	Tipperary (N. Riding)
FJ	Exeter	....	Exeter
FK	Worcester	....	Dudley
FL	Huntingdon &	....	
	Peterborough 65—	....	Peterborough
	Peterborough —65	....	
FM	Chester	....	Chester
FN	Canterbury	....	Canterbury
FO	Radnorshire	....	Hereford
FP	Rutland	....	Leicester
FR	Blackpool	....	Preston
FS	Edinburgh	....	Edinburgh
FT	Tynemouth	....	Newcastle upon Tyne
FU	Lindsey (Lincs.)	....	Grimsby
FV	Blackpool	....	Preston
FW	LIndsey (Lincs.)	....	Lincoln
FX	Dorset	....	Bournemouth
FY	Southport	....	Liverpool
FZ	Central Office Coleraine	....	Belfast

	Up to Sept. 1974	Write the registration you saw in full in this column	After Oct. 1974
G	Glasgow	....	—
GA	Glasgow	....	Glasgow
GB	Glasgow	....	Glasgow
GC	London	....	London S.W.
GD	Glasgow	....	Glasgow
GE	Glasgow	....	Glasgow
GF	London	....	London S.W.
GG	Glasgow	....	Glasgow
GH	London	....	London S.W.
GJ	London	....	London S.W.
GK	London	....	London S.W.
GL	Bath	....	Truro
GM	Motherwell & Wishaw	....	Reading
GN	London	....	London S.W.
GO	London	....	London S.W.
GP	London	....	London S.W.
GR	Sunderland	....	Durham
GS	Perthshire	....	Luton
GT	London	....	London S.W.
GU	London	....	London S.E.
GV	West Suffolk	....	Ipswich
GW	London	....	London S.E.
GX	London	....	London S.E.
GY	London	....	London S.E.
GZ	Central Office Coleraine	....	Belfast

IF YOU DON'T BELIEVE IN COINCIDENCES YOU WILL AFTER HEARING THIS!

The owner of a Mini acquired the registration 9 SWL for it, because it fitted his initials. He was driving along one day and just happened to glance at the plate on a car passing in the opposite direction. Not only was the number the reverse of his—SWL 9, but the car was a Mini too! He turned, caught up the car, and persuaded its owner to sell it (he was glad to—it was falling apart anyway!).

	Up to Sept. 1974	Write the registration you saw in full in this column	After Oct. 1974
H	Middlesex —65	....	—
HA	Warley 66—	....	Dudley
	Smethwick —66	....	
HB	Merthyr Tydfil	....	Cardiff
HC	Eastbourne	....	Hastings
HD	Dewsbury	....	Huddersfield
HE	Barnsley	....	Sheffield
HF	Wallasey	....	Liverpool
HG	Burnley	....	Preston
HH	Carlisle	....	Carlisle
HI	Tipperary (S. Riding)	....	Tipperary (S.R.)
HJ	Southend-on-Sea	....	Chelmsford
HK	Essex	....	Chelmsford
HL	Wakefield	....	Sheffield
HM	London 65—	....	London Central
	East Ham —65	....	
HN	Darlington	....	Middlesbrough
HO	Hampshire	....	Salisbury
HP	Coventry	....	Coventry
HR	Wiltshire	....	Swindon
HS	Renfrewshire	....	Glasgow
HT	Bristol	....	Bristol
HU	Bristol	....	Bristol
HV	London 65—	....	London Central
	East Ham —65	....	
HW	Bristol	....	Bristol
HX	London 65—	....	London Central
	Middlesex —65	....	
HY	Bristol	....	Bristol
HZ	Central Office Coleraine	....	Tyrone

	Up to Sept. 1974	Write the registration you saw in full in this column	After Oct. 1974
IA	Central Office Coleraine	....	Antrim
IB	Central Office Coleraine	....	Armagh
IC	Carlow	....	Carlow
ID	Cavan	....	Cavan
IE	Clare	....	Clare
IF	Cork	....	Cork
IH	Donegal	....	Donegal
IJ	Central Office Coleraine	....	Down
IK	Dublin	....	Dublin
IL	Central Office Coleraine	....	Fermanagh
IM	Galway	....	Galway
IN	Kerry	....	Kerry
IO	Kildare	....	Kildare
IP	Kilkenny	....	Kilkenny
IR	Offaly	....	Offaly
IT	Leitrim	....	Leitrim
IU	Limerick	....	Limerick
IW	Central Office Coleraine	....	Londonderry
IX	Longford	....	Longford
IY	Louth	....	Louth
IZ	Mayo	....	Mayo

And here's another non-car registration, and in an unusual arrangement. Any ideas?—Look out, it's moving . . .

. . . Did you get it? A Chieftain tank of the British Army out on manoeuvres. The armed services have their own system for registering all their many and varied vehicles so, sorry, but you can't score for seeing them. Just mind your toes!

	Up to Sept. 1974	Write the registration you saw in full in this column	After Oct. 1974
J	Durham	....	Jersey
JA	Stockport	....	Manchester
JB	Berkshire	....	Reading
JC	Caernarvonshire	....	Bangor
JD	London 65—	....	London Central
	West Ham —65	....	
JE	Cambridgeshire &	....	
	Isle of Ely 65—	....	Cambridge
	Isle of Ely —65	....	
JF	Leicester	....	Leicester
JG	Canterbury	....	Canterbury
JH	Hertfordshire	....	Reading
JI	Central Office Coleraine	....	Tyrone
JJ	London	....	Canterbury
JK	Eastbourne	....	Hastings
JL	Holland (Lincs.)	....	Boston
JM	Westmorland	....	Reading
JN	Southend-on-Sea	....	Chelmsford
JO	Oxford	....	Oxford
JP	Wigan	....	Warrington
JR	Northumberland	....	Newcastle upon Tyne
JS	Ross & Cromarty	....	Stornoway
JT	Dorset	....	Bournemouth
JU	Leicestershire	....	Leicester
JV	Grimsby	....	Grimsby
JW	Wolverhampton	....	Birmingham
JX	Halifax	....	Huddersfield
JY	Plymouth	....	Plymouth
JZ	Central Office Coleraine	....	Down

Up to Sept. 1974		Write the registration you saw in full in this column	After Oct. 1974
K	Liverpool	....	—
KA	Liverpool	....	Liverpool
KB	Liverpool	....	Liverpool
KC	Liverpool	....	Liverpool
KD	Liverpool	....	Liverpool
KE	Kent	....	Maidstone
KF	Liverpool	....	Liverpool
KG	Cardiff	....	Cardiff
KH	Kingston-upon-Hull	....	Kingston-upon-Hull
KI	Waterford	....	Waterford
KJ	Kent	....	Maidstone
KK	Kent	....	Maidstone
KL	Kent	....	Maidstone
KM	Kent	....	Maidstone
KN	Kent	....	Maidstone
KO	Kent	....	Maidstone
KP	Kent	....	Maidstone
KR	Kent	....	Maidstone
KS	Roxburghshire	....	Selkirk 75—
		....	St Boswell's —75
KT	Kent	....	Canterbury
KU	Bradford	....	Sheffield
KV	Coventry	....	Coventry
KW	Bradford	....	Sheffield
KX	Buckinghamshire	....	Luton
KY	Bradford	....	Sheffield
KZ	Central Office Coleraine	....	Antrim

Two names from show business with distinctive numbers: Jimmy Tarbuck has COM1C, and Tommy Steele has RAD10.

Up to Sept. 1974		Write the registration you saw in full in this column	After Oct. 1974
L	Glamorganshire	....	—
LA	London	....	London N.W.
LB	London	....	London N.W.
LC	London	....	London N.W.
LD	London	....	London N.W.
LE	London	....	London N.W.
LF	London	....	London N.W.
LG	Cheshire	....	Chester
LH	London	....	London N.W.
LI	Westmeath	....	Westmeath
LJ	Bournemouth	....	Bournemouth
LK	London	....	London N.W.
LL	London	....	London N.W.
LM	London	....	London N.W.
LN	London	....	London N.W.
LO	London	....	London N.W.
LP	London	....	London N.W.
LR	London	....	London N.W.
LS	Selkirkshire	....	Stirling
LT	London	....	London N.W.
LU	London	....	London N.W.
LV	Liverpool	....	Liverpool
LW	London	....	London N.W.
LX	London	....	London N.W.
LY	London	....	London N.W.
LZ	Central Office Coleraine	....	Armagh

Reflective plates were introduced in December 1967. A front plate must consist of black digits on a white reflective background and a back plate must have black digits on a yellow reflective background.

	Up to Sept. 1974	Write the registration you saw in full in this column	After Oct. 1974
M	Cheshire	....	—
MA	Cheshire	....	Chester
MB	Cheshire	....	Chester
MC	London 65— / Middlesex —65	....	London N.E.
MD		....	London N.E.
ME		....	London N.E.
MF		....	London N.E.
MG		....	London N.E.
MH		....	London N.E.
MI	Wexford	....	Wexford
MJ	Bedfordshire	....	Luton
MK	London 65— / Middlesex —65	....	London N.E.
ML		....	London N.E.
MM		....	London N.E.
MO	Berkshire	....	Reading
MP	London 65—	....	London N.E.
	Middlesex —65	....	
MR	Wiltshire	....	Swindon
MS	Stirlingshire	....	Stirling
MT	London 65— / Middlesex —65	....	London N.E.
MU		....	London N.E.
MV	London 65—	....	London S.E.
	Middlesex —65	....	
MW	Wiltshire	....	Swindon
MX	London 65— / Middlesex—65	....	London S.E.
MY		....	London S.E.
MZ	Central Office Coleraine	....	Belfast

	Up to Sept. 1974	Write the registration you saw in full in this column	After Oct. 1974
N	Manchester	....	—
NA	Manchester	....	Manchester
NB	Manchester	....	Manchester
NC	Manchester	....	Manchester
ND	Manchester	....	Manchester
NE	Manchester	....	Manchester
NF	Manchester	....	Manchester
NG	Norfolk	....	Norwich
NH	Northampton	....	Northampton
NI	Wicklow	....	Wicklow
NJ	East Sussex	....	Brighton
NK	Hertfordshire	....	Luton
NL	Northumberland	....	Newcastle upon Tyne
NM	Bedfordshire	....	Luton
NN	Nottinghamshire	....	Nottingham
NO	Essex	....	Chelmsford
NP	Worcestershire	....	Worcester
NR	Leicestershire	....	Leicester
NS	Sutherland	....	Glasgow
NT	Shropshire	....	Shrewsbury
NU	Derbyshire	....	Nottingham
NV	Northamptonshire	....	Northampton
NW	Leeds	....	Leeds
NX	Warwickshire	....	Dudley
NY	Glamorganshire	....	Cardiff
NZ	Central Office Coleraine	....	Londonderry

	Up to Sept. 1974	Write the registration you saw in full in this column	After Oct. 1974
O	Birmingham	....	—
OA	Birmingham	....	Birmingham
OB	Birmingham	....	Birmingham
OC	Birmingham	....	Birmingham
OD	Devonshire	....	Exeter
OE	Birmingham	....	Birmingham
OF	Birmingham	....	Birmingham
OG	Birmingham	....	Birmingham
OH	Birmingham	....	Birmingham
OJ	Birmingham	....	Birmingham
OI	Belfast	....	Belfast
OK	Birmingham	....	Birmingham
OL	Birmingham	....	Birmingham
OM	Birmingham	....	Birmingham
ON	Birmingham	....	Birmingham
OO	Essex	....	Chelmsford
OP	Birmingham	....	Birmingham
OR	Hampshire	....	Portsmouth
OS	Wigtownshire	....	Stranraer
OT	Hampshire	....	Portsmouth
OU	Hampshire	....	Bristol
OV	Birmingham	....	Birmingham
OW	Southampton	....	Portsmouth
OX	Birmingham	....	Birmingham
OY	London 65—	....	London N.W.
	Croydon —65	....	
OZ	Belfast	....	Belfast

	Up to Sept. 1974	Write the registration you saw in full in this column	After Oct. 1974
P	Surrey	....	—
PA	Surrey	....	Guildford
PB	Surrey	....	Guildford
PC	Surrey	....	Guildford
PD	Surrey	....	Guildford
PE	Surrey	....	Guildford
PF	Surrey	....	Guildford
PG	Surrey	....	Guildford
PH	Surrey	....	Guildford
PI	Cork	....	Cork
PJ	Surrey	....	Guildford
PK	Surrey	....	Guildford
PL	Surrey	....	Guildford
PM	East Sussex	....	Guildford
PN	East Sussex	....	Brighton
PO	West Sussex	....	Portsmouth
PP	Buckinghamshire	....	Luton
PR	Dorset	....	Bournemouth
PS	Zetland (Shetland Is.)	....	Lerwick (Shetland Is.)
PT	Durham	....	Durham
PU	Essex	....	Chelmsford
PV	Ipswich	....	Ipswich
PW	Norfolk	....	Norwich
PX	West Sussex	....	Portsmouth
PY	Yorkshire	....	Middlesbrough
PZ	Central Office Coleraine	....	Belfast

	Up to Sept. 1974	Write the registration you saw in full in this column	After Oct. 1974
QA	Greater London	....	London Central
QB	Greater London	....	London Central
QC	Greater London	....	London Central
QD	Greater London	....	London Central
QE	Greater London	....	London Central
QF	Greater London	....	London Central
QG	Greater London	....	London Central
QH	Greater London	....	London Central
QJ	Greater London	....	London Central
QK	Greater London	....	London Central
QL	Greater London	....	London Central
QM	Greater London	....	London Central
QN	Greater London	....	London Central
QP	Greater London	....	London Central
QQ	Greater London	....	London Central
QR	Greater London	....	London Central
QS	Greater London	....	London Central
QT	Greater London	....	London Central
QU	Greater London	....	London Central
QV	Greater London	....	London Central
QW	Greater London	....	London Central
QX	Greater London	....	London Central
QY	Greater London	....	London Central

An aptly numbered 1968 AC Cobra. This was the most powerful roadster ever built, with over 700 bhp under the bonnet!

The ultimate number plate! It is owned by the Rolls-Royce agents H. R. Owen Ltd.

	Up to Sept. 1974	Write the registration you saw in full in this column	After Oct. 1974
R	Derbyshire	....	—
RA	Derbyshire	....	Nottingham
RB	Derbyshire	....	Nottingham
RC	Derby	....	Nottingham
RD	Reading	....	Reading
RE	Staffordshire	....	Stoke-on-Trent
RF	Staffordshire	....	Stoke-on-Trent
RG	Aberdeen	....	Newcastle upon Tyne
RH	Kingston-upon-Hull	....	Kingston-upon-Hull
RI	Dublin	....	Dublin
RJ	Salford	....	Manchester
RK	London 65—	....	London N.W.
	Croydon —65	....	
RL	Cornwall	....	Truro
RM	Cumberland	....	Carlisle
RN	Preston	....	Preston
RO	Hertfordshire	....	Luton
RP	Northamptonshire	....	Northampton
RR	Nottinghamshire	....	Nottingham
RS	Aberdeen	....	Aberdeen
RT	East Suffolk	....	Ipswich
RU	Bournemouth	....	Bournemouth
RV	Portsmouth	....	Portsmouth
RW	Coventry	....	Coventry
RX	Berkshire	....	Reading
RY	Leicester	....	Leicester
RZ	Central Office Coleraine	....	Antrim

	Up to Sept. 1974	Write the registration you saw in full in this column	After Oct. 1974
S	Edinburgh	....	—
SA	Aberdeenshire	....	Aberdeen
SB	Argyllshire	....	Oban
SC	Edinburgh	....	Edinburgh
SD	Ayrshire	....	Ayr
SE	Banffshire	....	Keith
SF	Edinburgh	....	Edinburgh
SG	Edinburgh	....	Edinburgh
SH	Berwickshire	....	Selkirk 75—
		....	St Boswell's —75
SJ	Buteshire	....	Ayr
SK	Caithness	....	Wick
SL	Clackmannanshire	....	Dundee
SM	Dumfriesshire	....	Dumfries
SN	Dunbartonshire	....	Dundee
SO	Morayshire	....	Aberdeen
SP	Fifeshire	....	Dundee
SR	Angus	....	Dundee
SS	East Lothian	....	Aberdeen
ST	Inverness-shire	....	Inverness
SU	Kincardineshire	....	Glasgow
SV	Kinross-shire	....	—
SW	Kirkcudbrightshire	....	Dumfries
SX	West Lothian	....	Edinburgh
SY	Midlothian	....	—
SZ	Central Office Coleraine	....	Down

A guessing game with number plates. Look out for a car registration that spells something, and think what vehicle it would look best on. This one?—Look over the page . . .!

. . . there! Space below for your own sightings and solutions.

	Up to Sept. 1974	Write the registration you saw in full in this column	After Oct. 1974
T	Devonshire	....	—
TA	Devonshire	....	Exeter
TB	Lancashire	....	Warrington
TC	Lancashire	....	Bristol
TD	Lancashire	....	Bolton
TE	Lancashire	....	Bolton
TF	Lancashire	....	Reading
TG	Glamorganshire	....	Cardiff
TH	Carmarthenshire	....	Swansea
TI	Limerick	....	Limerick
TJ	Lancashire	....	Liverpool
TK	Dorset	....	Plymouth
TL	Kesteven (Lincs.)	....	Lincoln
TM	Bedfordshire	....	Luton
TN	Newcastle upon Tyne	....	Newcastle upon Tyne
TO	Nottingham	....	Nottingham
TP	Portsmouth	....	Portsmouth
TR	Southampton	....	Portsmouth
TS	Dundee	....	Dundee
TT	Devonshire	....	Exeter
TU	Cheshire	....	Chester
TV	Nottingham	....	Nottingham
TW	Essex	....	Chelmsford
TX	Glamorganshire	....	Cardiff
TY	Northumberland	....	Newcastle upon Tyne
TZ	Central Office Coleraine	....	Belfast

	Up to Sept. 1974	Write the registration you saw in full in this column	After Oct. 1974
U	Leeds	....	—
UA	Leeds	....	Leeds
UB	Leeds	....	Leeds
UC	London	....	London Central
UD	Oxfordshire	....	Oxford
UE	Warwickshire	....	Dudley
UF	Brighton	....	Brighton
UG	Leeds	....	Leeds
UH	Cardiff	....	Cardiff
UI	Central Office Coleraine	....	Londonderry
UJ	Shropshire	....	Shrewsbury
UK	Wolverhampton	....	Birmingham
UL	London	....	London Central
UM	Leeds	....	Leeds
UN	Denbighshire	....	Barnstaple
UO	Devonshire	....	Barnstaple
UP	Durham	....	Durham
UR	Hertfordshire	....	Luton
US	Glasgow 12—	....	Glasgow
	Govan —12	....	
UT	Leicestershire	....	Leicester
UU	London	....	London Central
UV	London	....	London Central
UW	London	....	London Central
UX	Shropshire	....	Shrewsbury
UY	Worcestershire	....	Worcester
UZ	Central Office Coleraine	....	Belfast

Proof that numbers change cars. In the last **I-SPY Car Numbers** MAD 1 was on an Aston Martin *above.* Now look where it has gone!

Cherished number on a cherished car, the 1951 Jaguar XK120.

'525 miles per gallon'?—a likely story!

	Up to Sept. 1974	Write the registration you saw in full in this column	After Oct. 1974
V	Lanarkshire	....	—
VA	Lanarkshire	....	Cambridge
VB	London 65—	....	Canterbury
	Croydon —65	....	
VC	Coventry	....	Coventry
VD	Lanarkshire	....	Luton
VE	Cambridgeshire &	....	
	Isle of Ely 65—	....	Cambridge
	Cambridgeshire —65	....	
VF	Norfolk	....	Norwich
VG	Norwich	....	Norwich
VH	Huddersfield	....	Huddersfield
VJ	Herefordshire	....	Hereford
VK	Newcastle upon Tyne	....	Newcastle upon Tyne
VL	Lincoln	....	Lincoln
VM	Manchester	....	Manchester
VN	Yorkshire N.R.	....	Middlesbrough
VO	Nottinghamshire	....	Nottingham
VP	Birmingham	....	Birmingham
VR	Manchester	....	Manchester
VS	Greenock	....	Luton
VT	Stoke-on-Trent	....	Stoke-on-Trent
VU	Manchester	....	Manchester
VV	Northampton	....	Northampton
VW	Essex	....	Chelmsford
VX	Essex	....	Chelmsford
VY	York	....	York
VZ	Central Office Coleraine	....	Tyrone

	Up to Sept. 1974	Write the registration you saw in full in this column	After Oct. 1974
W	Sheffield	....	—
WA	Sheffield	....	Sheffield
WB	Sheffield	....	Sheffield
WC	Essex	....	Chelmsford
WD	Warwickshire	....	Dudley
WE	Sheffield	....	Sheffield
WF	Yorkshire E.R.	....	Sheffield
WG	Stirlingshire	....	Sheffield
WH	Bolton	....	Bolton
WI	Waterford	....	Waterford
WJ	Sheffield	....	Sheffield
WK	Coventry	....	Coventry
WL	Oxford	....	Oxford
WM	Southport	....	Liverpool
WN	Swansea	....	Swansea
WO	Monmouthshire	....	Cardiff
WP	Worcestershire	....	Worcester
WR	Yorkshire W.R.	....	Leeds
WS	Edinburgh 20—	....	Bristol
	Leith —20	....	
WT	Yorkshire W.R.	....	Leeds
WU	Yorkshire W.R.	....	Leeds
WV	Wiltshire	....	Brighton
WW	Yorkshire N.R.	....	Leeds
WX	Yorkshire N.R.	....	Leeds
WY	Yorkshire N.R.	....	Leeds
WZ	Central Office Coleraine	....	Belfast